THIS CANDLEWICK BIOGRAPHY BELONGS TO:

"[A young inventor's] first endeavors are purely instinctive, promptings of an imagination vivid and undisciplined. As we grow older reason asserts itself and we become more and more systematic and designing. But those early impulses, though not immediately productive, are of the greatest moment and may shape our very destinies."

—NIKOLA TESLA

ELECTRICAL WIZARD

HOW NIKOLA TESLA LIT UP THE WORLD

ROCKFORD PUBLIC LIBRARY

ELIZABETH RUSCH   *illustrated by* OLIVER DOMINGUEZ

CANDLEWICK PRESS

For Cobi and Izzi
E. R.

To my wife, Melissa Dominguez
O. D.

First edition in this format 2015

Library of Congress Catalog Card Number 2012954334
ISBN 978-0-7636-5855-7 (hardcover)
ISBN 978-0-7636-7978-1 (reformatted hardcover)
ISBN 978-0-7636-7979-8 (reformatted paperback)

15 16 17 18 19 20 APS 10 9 8 7 6 5 4 3 2 1

Printed in Humen, Dongguan, China

This book was typeset in Adobe Caslon.
The illustrations were done in graphite, gouache, acrylic, and ink on paper.

Candlewick Press
99 Dover Street
Somerville, Massachusetts 02144

visit us at www.candlewick.com

TABLE OF CONTENTS

CHAPTER ONE

THE NIGHT OF Nikola Tesla's birth, lightning zapped, crackled, and flashed overhead. For years after, booming thunder drew the poor Serbian boy to the window of his family's small house. Nikola gazed, mystified, as electrical bolts ricocheted across the sky.

One evening, when he was three, Nikola stroked his cat, Macak. The cat's fur snapped with tiny sparks. "What is it?" Nikola wondered. Was it some kind of wizardry?

"Electricity," his father explained, "the same thing you see through the trees in a storm."

Enchanted by the sparking halo his hands had conjured, Nikola wondered what other magic he could perform.

When he was five, Nikola dangled his fingers in a nearby brook. How fast the water moved! How hard it pushed his hand! Nikola had an idea. He found a disk cut from a tree trunk. He poked a hole in the disk, jammed a stick through the hole, then balanced the wheel above the stream. The wooden wheel spun and spun as if under the spell of the water.

Nikola began to notice invisible energy everywhere. Even the flight of insects thrummed with power. When he was nine, he built a propeller spun by flying June bugs. "Once they were started," he marveled, "they continued whirling for hours and hours."

As a teenager, Nikola became entranced by a photograph of Niagara Falls' cascading waters. As he remembered his little creek waterwheel, a vision flashed into his mind. He imagined giant waterwheels, pummeled by Niagara's pounding waters, spinning endlessly.

Nikola made a prophecy: *Someday, I will turn the power of Niagara Falls into electricity.*

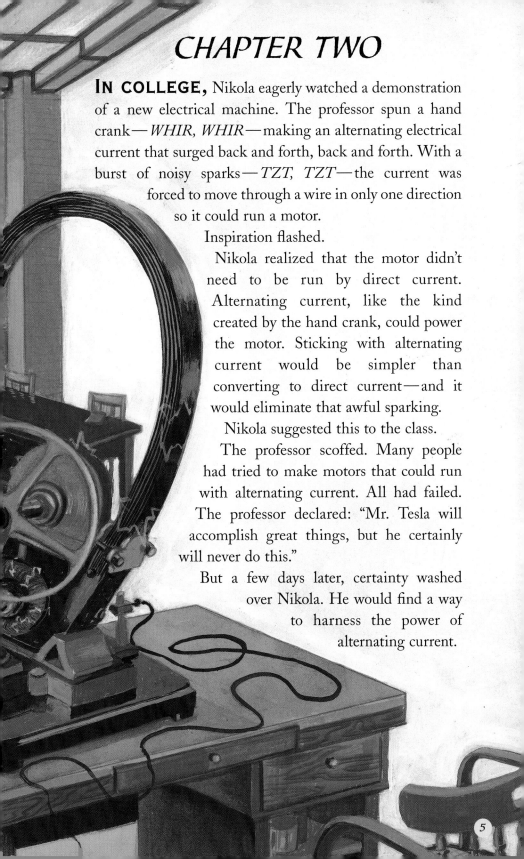

CHAPTER TWO

IN COLLEGE, Nikola eagerly watched a demonstration of a new electrical machine. The professor spun a hand crank—*WHIR, WHIR*—making an alternating electrical current that surged back and forth, back and forth. With a burst of noisy sparks—*TZT, TZT*—the current was forced to move through a wire in only one direction so it could run a motor.

Inspiration flashed.

Nikola realized that the motor didn't need to be run by direct current. Alternating current, like the kind created by the hand crank, could power the motor. Sticking with alternating current would be simpler than converting to direct current—and it would eliminate that awful sparking.

Nikola suggested this to the class.

The professor scoffed. Many people had tried to make motors that could run with alternating current. All had failed. The professor declared: "Mr. Tesla will accomplish great things, but he certainly will never do this."

But a few days later, certainty washed over Nikola. He would find a way to harness the power of alternating current.

The problem of alternating current hummed in
Nikola's mind. He took a job climbing telephone
poles in Budapest and imagined electrical current
that surged back and forth, back and forth.

He invented a loudspeaker for phones and imagined electrical current that surged back and forth, back and forth.

He moved to Paris, where he worked on electrical devices designed by American inventor Thomas Edison—generators, motors, fuses, and switches—and imagined electrical current that surged back and forth, back and forth.

CHAPTER THREE

ONE DAY, when he was twenty-six, Nikola went for a walk with a friend. The sun set in a fiery blaze.

The buzzing thoughts inside Nikola's head sparked together like a lightning bolt.

Suddenly he understood how to power a motor using alternating current! He saw it all clearly in his mind.

Nikola grabbed a stick, waving it like a wand. "See how smoothly it is running?" he gasped. "There is no sparking."

"I see nothing," said his friend. "The sun is not sparking. Are you ill?"

Nikola dropped to his knees and began drawing a diagram in the dirt. At last his companion understood how alternating current could spin a motor using magnets whose poles flipped back and forth, back and forth.

Over the next few months, Nikola conjured in his head all the parts of a new electrical system based on alternating current. Night and day, Nikola pictured the machines, designing, testing, and fixing problems he saw. He didn't have to write anything down. He could see it all in his mind.

Nikola traveled through Europe, seeking money to build his AC machines. He felt like a fortune-teller. The days of candlelight, gas lamps, and direct current were over, he told investors. Not only could alternating current power lights and motors, but it could also travel great distances much more cheaply and efficiently than direct current. It could power every house, every business, everything from tiny lightbulbs to huge factories.

No one believed him.

So he sailed to America, where he knew of at least one person who would be interested in his ideas: Thomas Edison.

CHAPTER FOUR

TWO DAYS after docking in New York City, Nikola Tesla stepped into the office of his hero. Nikola handed Edison a letter of recommendation, written by a mutual friend. It said:

I know two great men and you are one of them; the other is this young man.

"What can you do?" Edison asked.

Nikola burst into a description of how alternating current could power the world.

"Nonsense." Edison scowled. "We're set up for direct current in America. People like it, and it's all I'll ever fool with."

Instead of becoming Nikola's partner in electrifying the world, Edison became his greatest rival.

Nikola was desperate for money to build his inventions. He invited bankers, business bigwigs, and powerful people like author Mark Twain to his darkened lab for strange demonstrations of the wonders of alternating current.

In one demonstration, Nikola held out a simple glass tube.

With his other hand, he reached for a wire. "I bring my body in contact with a wire conveying alternating currents. . . ."

The audience squirmed at the thought of the shock.

When Nikola's hand touched the wire, the tube glowed!

Nikola spun slowly so everyone could see that the electrical current traveled across his body to the tube.

Then Nikola released the wire and strode away. The tube still coursed with light.

The audience gaped in awe: How did the electricity get to the bulb without any wires?

"Is there, I ask, can there be, a more interesting study than that of alternating currents?" he asked his audience.

CHAPTER FIVE

OVER TIME, Nikola's fame grew, until he raised enough money to build his AC generators and motors. Tesla quickly got to work. He recreated the machines exactly as he had imagined them. As he predicted, they worked perfectly.

But Tesla's joy was short lived. His old rival, Thomas Edison, who already ran a dozen direct-current power stations, moved fast to squelch the competition. He blanketed New York with pamphlets. Alternating current is dangerous, he warned, even deadly. To prove his point, Edison's associates electrocuted dogs, horses, and even an elephant with alternating current. Direct current is just as deadly, but no one mentioned this in the demonstrations. Edison wouldn't rest until investors and the public alike were scared away from Nikola's new technology.

At the height of the "war of the currents" came the biggest electrical challenge in history. The Chicago World's Fair was to be the first ever fair lit with electricity.

People assumed Edison would get the job of wiring the fair. To everyone's surprise, the company Westinghouse, which would use Nikola's inventions, won the honor.

But could they do it? Would Nikola's mysterious inventions safely provide enough electricity to illuminate the entire fair? What if there was so much electricity that a fire started or part of the fair blew up?

On opening day, people flooded the fairgrounds. They wandered through the alabaster buildings, gawked at the first Ferris wheel, and flocked to taste strange new foods: Shredded Wheat cereal, Cracker Jack, and Juicy Fruit gum.

In the Great Hall of Electricity, people gaped over electric lamps, elevators, fans, sewing machines, stoves, and laundry machines, all run with alternating current.

But the true test of the electrical system would happen at sunset. As day ended and night darkened the sky, the president of the United States, Grover Cleveland, turned a golden key. . . .

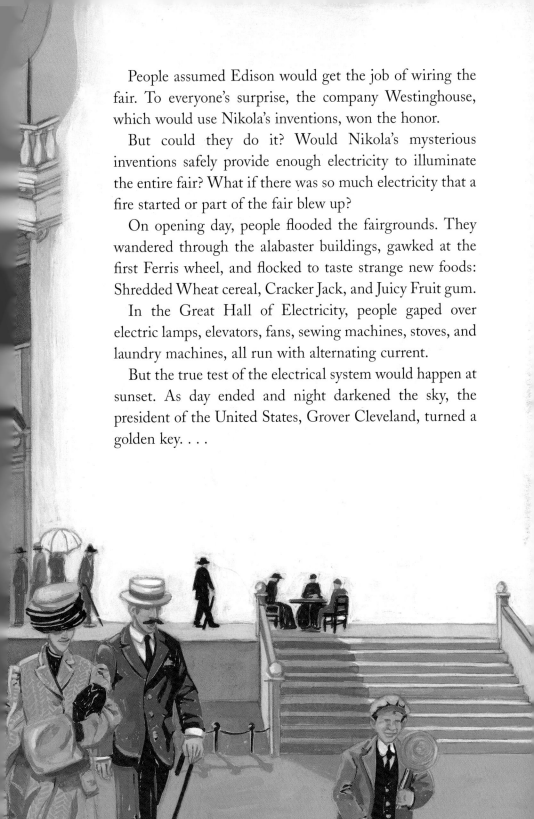

FLASH! All at once, 100,000 lamps illuminated the fairgrounds, creating a spectacle of light never before seen anywhere in the world. The crowd went wild.

IT WAS A MIRACLE!

IT WAS LIKE MAGIC!

CHAPTER SIX

BACK IN THE Great Hall of Electricity, Nikola stepped onto a stage. Tall, elegant, and proud, he grabbed the end of a wire and flicked a switch. More than 250,000 volts of electricity pulsed across his body, tingling his muscles. The crowd pressed back in alarm, expecting him to be burned or even to die.

But Nikola was very much alive. Glimmering in a halo of sparks, he was a marvelous sight to behold. "Wonders baffling explanation we now see in a different light," Nikola exclaimed.

The fair had been a triumph, but Nikola had an even more astounding trick up his sleeve. The pulsing, ground-quaking waters of Niagara Falls had haunted him for years. He couldn't shake from his mind the picture of Niagara's pounding water rotating huge wheels, which would spin huge magnets, generating electricity for thousands of homes.

Vanishing from the limelight, Nikola toiled for two years to turn his vision of spinning wheels into the most gigantic electrical project ever attempted. No one was sure if it would work. No one except Nikola Tesla, who could picture it all in his mind.

CHAPTER SEVEN

FINALLY the first huge generator was ready. With a sleight of hand, an engineer diverted Niagara's gushing water toward the turbines. An aluminum factory roared to life.

A year later, more turbines and generators joined the throng. Houses shimmered with light.

Electricity reached Buffalo, New York, twenty-two miles away. Railway cars surged forward.

"I saw my boyhood plan carried out," Nikola marveled, "and wondered at the unfathomable mystery of the mind."

Nikola's miraculous inventions at Niagara soon electrified the trolleys, subways, and great buildings of New York City—even the blinding lights of Broadway. Not long after, electricity spread to homes and businesses across America.

Eventually, Nikola Tesla's electrical wizardry illuminated the world.

And it all started with a spark.

Ahead of His Time

Nikola Tesla's ideas were so revolutionary, so ahead of their time, that we are only now realizing how his work has transformed our world. If you play with a remote-control car, flick on a fluorescent or neon light, get an X-ray to see if your arm is broken, check the speedometer in a car, call someone on a cell phone, or even just turn on the radio, you are using Nikola Tesla's inventions.

While developing his AC electrical system, Tesla was also in hot pursuit of wireless transmission. In 1898, he demonstrated the first remote control. In a large tank of water, he floated a gigantic toy boat, five feet long by three feet wide. From a device in his hand, he moved the boat forward and back, left and right, and turned its light on and off. Observers asked to see inside the boat—they thought someone must be inside controlling it.

Tesla soon developed ways to transmit signals long distances without wires. But another inventor stole his wireless thunder. In 1901, Italian Guglielmo Marconi transmitted and received radio signals across the Atlantic Ocean. Three years later, Marconi was awarded a patent for the radio. But the Italian's work was based on as many as seventeen of Nikola Tesla's patents. (In 1943, the U.S. Supreme Court ruled that Nikola Tesla was in fact the inventor of the radio.)

In the spring of 1899, Tesla stepped off a train at Colorado Springs to embark on his most ambitious wireless project ever: to transmit not signals but *electricity* without wires. Electrical waves he detected during a lightning storm had convinced him that it would be possible to "transmit power, in unlimited amounts, to any terrestrial distance and almost without loss." He managed to make 130-foot-long sparks before blowing out the entire powerhouse for Colorado Springs.

In 1901, he tried again, building a strange giant tower called Wardenclyffe that he hoped would generate 7.5 million kilowatts and wrap the globe with wireless communication and nearly free electric power. But his investors pulled their funding before Tesla could test his idea. "If anyone can draw on the power, where do we put the meter?" complained financier J.P. Morgan.

Some of the inventor's ideas are still powerful enough to transform our world today. Nikola Tesla imagined robots that could think for themselves and electricity generated from the swell of tides. He even proposed harnessing the energy of spinning planets. "We are whirling through endless space with an inconceivable speed, all around us everything is spinning, everything is moving, everywhere is energy," he said. "There *must* be some way of availing ourselves of this energy more directly."

Maybe one day, with the help of your ideas and ingenuity, these ideas will become reality.

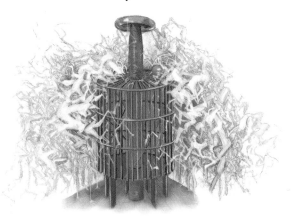

Tesla vs. Edison: The Rivalry

When Thomas Edison and Nikola Tesla first met in 1884, the American inventor had eighteen power stations producing direct-current electricity in New York, Boston, Philadelphia, and New Orleans — and plans for hundreds more. The renowned inventor was already the master of a new electrical empire.

Nikola Tesla was an unknown electrician with a strange accent whose only invention existed in his head. And Tesla's alternating-current idea wasn't an improvement of the direct-current system; it was a direct competitor.

Though Edison dismissed Tesla's ideas about alternating current, he did hire the young engineer. For a year, Nikola toiled for Edison, often from 10:30 a.m. until five the next morning. Edison said to him, "I have had many hardworking assistants but you take the cake."

He promised to pay Tesla $50,000 to improve his direct-current motors. Tesla did, but when he tried to collect his pay, Edison just laughed. "Tesla, you don't understand our American humor." Nikola stormed out of Edison's office. The young engineer struggled financially for months, even digging ditches to feed himself.

When Tesla found investors and began developing his AC electrical system, Edison strove to squelch the competition before it even got off the ground. He published a pamphlet with a scarlet cover blazoned with the word WARNING! that claimed that alternating current was deadly. "It is a matter of fact," he wrote, "that any system employing high pressure, i.e. 500 to 2,000 units [volts], jeopardizes life." He backed efforts to limit the voltage of current used in New York City (which would rid AC of its advantage), to electrocute animals with AC current, and to convince New York State to enforce the death penalty using an AC-powered electric chair.

Even after Edison lost the contract to wire the World's Fair, he continued to put up a fight. Edison barred Westinghouse from using his incandescent lightbulb design at the fair. While scrambling to install the biggest lighting system in history, the Westinghouse team had to invent a new lightbulb, build a glass factory, and produce a quarter million of the new bulbs. Despite Edison's roadblocks, Tesla and Westinghouse succeeded brilliantly.

One later incident suggests a grudging respect between the two inventors. In 1895, Nikola Tesla's lab was completely destroyed by a fire. Edison let Tesla use his equipment and work in his lab for a few weeks until he got a new lab up and running.

In 1917, Nikola Tesla was offered what had become the most prestigious award in electrical engineering, the Edison Medal. At first Nikola refused. "You would not be honoring Tesla," he wrote, "but Edison, who has previously shared unearned glory from every previous recipient of this medal." But eventually, Tesla accepted.

The night of the award ceremony, a friend introduced Nikola Tesla: "Were we to seize and eliminate from our industrial world the results of Mr. Tesla's work, the wheels of industry would cease to turn, our electric cars and trains would stop, our towns would be dark."

While Thomas Edison himself never publicly recognized the genius of Nikola Tesla's work, the honor given in his name did.

Scientific Notes

WARNING: ELECTRICITY KILLS! Electricity of any kind—alternating current or direct current—can be dangerous and deadly. If you touch a live wire, you become part of the electrical circuit, with current racing through all your body parts. Moisture of any kind—humidity in the air, sweat, pool or bath water—helps electricity get inside your body easily. Even a small amount of electricity can stop your heart from beating. Electricity flowing through your body also encounters resistance, which turns the electricity into heat. An electrical shock literally fries your insides.

You should NEVER fool around with electricity, stick anything other than a proper plug in an electrical socket, or go anywhere near a downed electrical wire. Any electrical experiments you do *must* be closely supervised by a responsible adult. Your life depends on it.

What Happened to Macak the Cat?

Everything is made of atoms, with electrons zooming around their edges. Most of the time, electrons stay with their own atom, but sometimes they leave one atom and jump to another. This movement of electrons is electricity.

Macak's sparks came from static electricity. As Macak rolled around on the floor, he picked up spare electrons from the rug. When Nikola reached out to pet his cat, the electrons quickly rushed from Macak's fur to Nikola's hand. *Zap!*

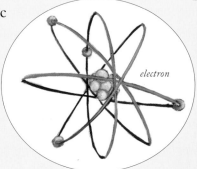

electron

What Is the Difference between AC and DC?

Current is the movement of electrons through a wire. In direct current, electrons move through a wire in only one direction. In alternating current, on the other hand, electrons move first in one direction and then the other, reversing their direction over and over.

When electrons travel through a wire, resistance generates heat. This heat is wasted energy. Using a higher voltage reduces these losses. But high voltage is also dangerous; this is why homes use a relatively low voltage (around 120 volts).

DC voltage can't be easily changed: Whatever level is generated must be used at the other end. Alternating current, though, can be transformed from low voltage to high voltage in order to travel hundreds of miles efficiently and then easily transformed again to any voltage needed for use in homes, businesses, and factories.

Thomas Edison's DC system required power stations every mile or so, generating low-voltage electricity that quickly lost energy as it traveled to nearby homes. Tesla's system allowed for larger energy generators to spread electricity more widely and efficiently.

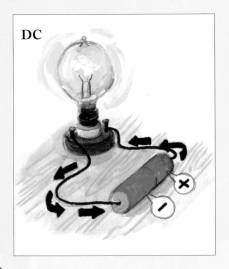

DC

AC

AC generator

How Does Spinning a Hand Crank Make Electricity?

The electrical machine Nikola Tesla saw in college was actually an electrical generator that transformed the spinning of the hand crank into electricity.

Here's how it works:

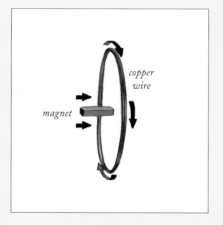

1. A magnet that moves near a wire causes electrons to flow within the wire. This is called inducing (or making) current.

2. The first electrical generators featured magnets that stayed still. Turning a hand crank spun a loop of wire in the space between two magnets.

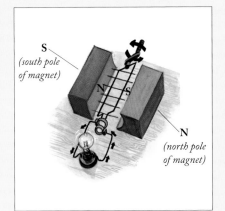

S
(south pole of magnet)

N

(north pole of magnet)

3. Spinning the wire loop through the fixed magnetic field caused electrons within the wire to flow in one direction, inducing current.

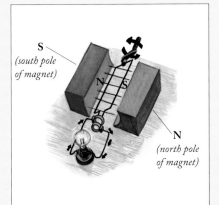

S
(south pole of magnet)

N

(north pole of magnet)

4. As the wire loop continued to spin, the direction of the electron flow was reversed.

electrical generator

5. With each half rotation of the wire loop, the current reversed direction, making what is called alternating current.

How Does Tesla's Amazing AC Motor Work?

Nikola Tesla knew that sending electricity through coils wrapped around metal would create temporary magnets. The poles of these "electromagnets" can be changed by reversing the direction of current flow through the coils. Tesla's AC motor uses electromagnets that are held in place and a regular magnet that is allowed to spin. When this magnet spins, it turns the motor.

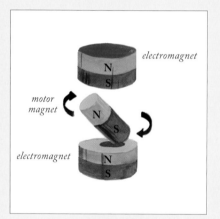

1. At first, the north pole of the motor magnet is pulled toward the south pole of one electromagnet while the south pole of the motor magnet is pulled toward the north pole of the other electromagnet.

2. The inside magnet turns until its north pole lines up with the magnetic field generated by the south poles of the electromagnets. (And the south pole of the inside magnet lines up with the magnetic field generated by the north poles of the electromagnet.)

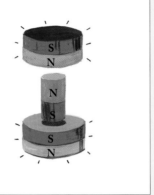

3. Then the alternating current flowing through the electro-magnets swaps their poles. Suddenly the magnetic fields are aligned with north next to north (N-N) and south next to south (S-S).

4. The poles are the same (N-N, S-S), so they push each other away, continuing the spin of the motor.

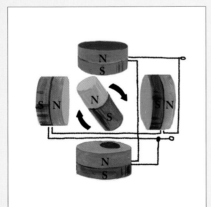

5. Tesla realized that he could get the motor spinning quickly and smoothly by using three or more electromagnets with their pole switches timed to pull the spinning magnet at just the right moments.

How Did Tesla Light a Bulb with His Hand?

Two of Tesla's inventions played important roles in this impressive experiment. The first was a machine called the Tesla Coil, which could take current that usually changed direction fifty or sixty times a second and force it to alternate thousands or even millions of times a second. This high-frequency alternating current created a field of harmless electricity in the air.

The second invention was a fluorescent light. The inside of a glass bulb—empty except for a little gas—was coated with a special powder. Electricity flowing through the bulb excited the gas within, which made the coating glow with light. In the demonstration, Tesla first conducted electricity from the wire, across his body, to the bulb. But he didn't really need the wire. When Tesla let go of the wire, he conducted electricity from the air to the bulb. But Tesla didn't even need to hold the bulb! While in the electrical field, fluorescent bulbs could even glow with no one holding them.

How Did Tesla Survive 250,000 Volts of Electricity?

The alternating current flowing through the wire to Tesla was changing direction at a very high frequency (millions of times a second). Very high-frequency currents have a quirk that kept Tesla safe: High-frequency currents travel along the outside of objects instead of penetrating through them. So instead of spreading through Tesla's body, the high-frequency current traveled along the surface of his skin. That protected his heart, which can seize up from even small amounts of current.

Harnessing Niagara

Capturing the power of Niagara Falls was trickier than just placing waterwheels under the falls. But the concept was the same. A construction company built long tunnels that started above the falls and dropped straight down. Engineers positioned turbines near the bottom of the tunnels. Water diverted from the river above poured down the tunnels and spun the turbines. A long, strong rod sticking up from the center of the turbine led to a generator in the powerhouse. The rod spun a rotor holding large magnets. As the magnets spun past a coil, they generated electricity.

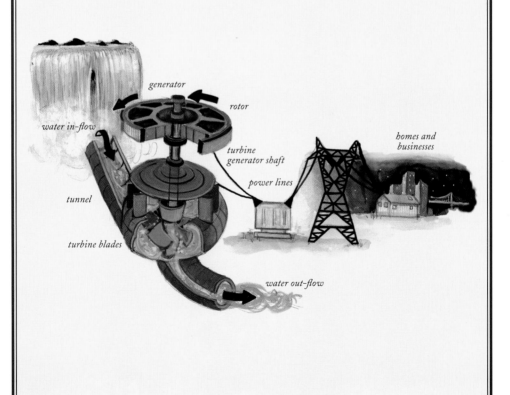

generator

rotor

water in-flow

turbine generator shaft

homes and businesses

tunnel

power lines

turbine blades

water out-flow

IMPORTANT DATES

1856   Nikola Tesla is born in the Austro-Hungarian village of Smiljan, Lika, to Serbian parents.

1875   Tesla enrolls at the Austrian Polytechnic School in Graz.

1881   Tesla goes to work as electrical engineer for a telegraph company in Budapest, Hungary.

1882   Tesla conceives of the idea of how to succssfully use alternating current (AC).

1884   Tesla emigrates to the U.S. and begins working with Thomas Edison.

1885   Tesla tenders his resignation with Thomas Edison.

1890   Tesla lights up a vacuum tube by transmitting energy through the air.

1891   Tesla invents Tesla Coil, which produces high-voltage, low-current, high-frequency AC electricity.

1891   Tesla becomes a U.S. citizen.

1893   AC is used to power the World's Fair (Columbian Exposition) in Chicago.

1896   The Niagara Falls Power Project sends electricity to Buffalo using AC.

1898   Tesla demonstrates the use of a remote-control device.

1916   Tesla receives the Edison Medal from the Institute of Electrical and Electronics Engineers (IEEE).

1943   Tesla dies in New York City.

1975   Tesla is inducted into the Inventors Hall of Fame.

SOURCE NOTES

"[A young inventor's] first endeavors . . . destinies": Tesla, *Treasury*, p. 619.

"Electricity . . . trees in a storm": Tesla, Nikola, "A Story of Youth Told by Age," 1939, reprinted in "Tesla: Master of Lightning," www.pbs.org.

"Once they were started . . . hours and hours": Tesla, Nikola, *My Inventions* (Austin: Hart Brothers, 1982), p. 45.

"Mr. Tesla will accomplish . . . never do this": O'Neill, p. 41.

"See how smoothly . . . no sparking" and "I see nothing. . . . Are you ill?" Ibid., p. 49.

"I know two great men . . . this young man": Ibid., p. 60.

"What can you do?" and "Nonsense. We're set up . . . all I'll ever fool with": quoted in Cheney, p. 53.

"I bring my body . . . alternating currents" and "Is there, I ask . . . alternating currents?": Tesla, *Treasury*, pp. 122 and 123.

"Wonders baffling explanation we now see in a different light": Tesla, Nikola, "Experiments with Alternate Currents of Very High Frequency and Their Application to Methods of Artificial Illumination," lecture at Columbia College, May 20, 1891, reported as the same demonstration he gave at the fair.

"I saw my boyhood plan . . . of the mind": quoted in *Tesla: Master of Lightning.*

"transmit power, in unlimited amounts . . . without loss": Tesla, Nikola, "The Transmission of Electrical Energy without Wires," *Electrical World and Engineer,* March 5, 1904.

"If anyone can draw on the power, where do we put the meter?": quoted in *Nikola Tesla: The Genius Who Lit the World.*

"We are whirling . . . more directly": quoted in Martin, Thomas Commerford, ed., *The Inventions, Researches, and Writings of Nikola Tesla* (New York: The Electrical Engineer, 1894), pp. 196–197.

"I have had many . . . take the cake": Tesla, *Treasury*, p. 645.

"Tesla, you don't understand our American humor": quoted in O'Neill, p. 64.

"It is a matter of fact . . . jeopardizes life": quoted in Jonnes, p. 152.

"You would not be honoring Tesla . . . recipient of this medal": quoted in Cheney, p. 268.

"Were we to seize and eliminate . . . would be dark": Ibid., p. 270.

SELECT BIBLIOGRAPHY & FURTHER READING

BIBLIOGRAPHY

Books

Primary Source

Tesla, Nikola. *The Nikola Tesla Treasury*. Radford, VA: Wilder, 2007.

Biographies

Cheney, Margaret. *Tesla: Man Out of Time*. New York: Touchstone, 2001.

Jonnes, Jill. *Empires of Light: Edison, Tesla, Westinghouse, and the Race to Electrify the World*. New York: Random House, 2003.

McNichol, Tom. *AC/DC: The Savage Tale of the First Standards War*. San Francisco: Jossey-Bass, 2006.

O'Neill, John J. *Prodigal Genius: The Life of Nikola Tesla*. New York: Cosimo Classics, 1944.

Seifer, Marc J. *Wizard: The Life and Times of Nikola Tesla, Biography of a Genius*. New York: Kensington Publishing, 1998.

Documentary Films

Nikola Tesla: The Genius Who Lit the World. UFO TV, 2004.

Mad Electricity. The History Channel, 2010.

Tesla: Master of Lightning. PBS, 2007.

FOR FURTHER READING

Aldrich, Lisa J. *Nikola Tesla and the Taming of Electricity*. Greensboro, N.C.: Morgan Reynolds, 2005.

MANY THANKS

Researching and writing about the genius Nikola Tesla required something close to getting a flash master's degree in history, biography, and electrical engineering. Deep thanks to my teachers and sounding boards: friend and engineer Vincent O'Malley; electrical engineer Adam Wilson; Jim Hardesty, PhD, a physics historian and founder of PV Scientific Instruments; and Nikola Lonchar, president of the Tesla Science Foundation.

For help in getting not just the science but the words right, I thank the critique group Viva Scriva—Addie Boswell, Ruth Feldman, Amber Keyser, Sabina Rascol, Mary Rehmann, and Nicole Schreiber—as well as the writers Nancy Coffelt, Kim Griswell, Barbara Kerley, editor Abigail Samoun, agent Kelly Sonnack, and assistant Tatty Bartholomew.

Finally, my deepest appreciation goes to editor Kaylan Adair for her boundless enthusiasm for her first-ever nonfiction project and to the team at Candlewick Press for their stellar work helping to distill the essence of this brilliant and quirky inventor into a children's book.

INDEX

ELIZABETH RUSCH is the author of numerous nonfiction books for young readers, including *The Mighty Mars Rovers; For the Love of Music: The Remarkable Story of Maria Anna Mozart; Volcano Rising;* and *The Planet Hunter: The Story Behind What Happened to Pluto.* About *Electrical Wizard,* she says, "The more I learned about Nikola Tesla while researching this book, the more I realized how completely this one inventor has shaped modern life." Elizabeth Rusch uses Nikola Tesla's inventions daily in her home in Portland, Oregon.

OLIVER DOMINGUEZ is a fine artist and illustrator of the picture book *Miracle Mud: Lena Blackburne and the Secret Mud that Changed Baseball* by David A. Kelly. About *Electrical Wizard,* he says, "Researching Nikola Tesla's life and the era in which he lived was a wonderful learning experience; it transported me to a world of the past I was unfamiliar with. Tesla was not only an amazing inventor but also a dreamer, way beyond his time. It taught me that perseverance and dreams should never be silenced and to always dream big." Oliver Dominguez lives in Fort Myers, Florida, with his wife, their daughter, and their two very animated chocolate Labs.